Why I Pray

By Doris A. Valentine

Copyright © 2021 Doris A. Valentine. All rights reserved. No part of this book may be used or reproduced in any form without express written permission from the publisher except for brief quotes, approved excerpts, articles, and reviews. For information, quotes from the author, or interview requests, contact the publisher.

Scriptures not marked are taken from the NEW KING JAMES VERSION (NKJV). Scriptures marked NKJV are taken from the NEW KING JAMES VERSION (NKJV): Scripture taken from the NEW KING JAMES VERSION®. Copyright© 1982 by Thomas Nelson, Inc. Used by permission. All rights reserved.

Scriptures marked NLT are taken from the HOLY BIBLE, NEW LIVING TRANSLATION (NLT): Scriptures taken from the HOLY BIBLE, NEW LIVING TRANSLATION, Copyright© 1996, 2004, 2007 by Tyndale House Foundation. Used by permission of Tyndale House Publishers, Inc., Carol Stream, Illinois 60188. All rights reserved. Used by permission.

Cover design by Jody Dyer

ISBN 978-1-970037-83-8

Library of Congress Control Number: 2019920462

Crippled Beagle Publishing
Knoxville, Tennessee, USA
www.crippledbeaglepublishing.com

Published and printed in the United States of America.

THIS BOOK IS DEDICATED to my father's baby brother, Private Burnette Lewelling, lovingly called "Little Bud" by his family of four sisters and three brothers. He was unmarried and worked on the farm like a lot of men did during this time. Burnette joined the military. He was only 26 years old when he died on September 10,1942, in India. The initial report and newspaper article said he lost his life in the line of duty. After several letters back and forth with military, the family learned that Burnette shot himself in the head. Military personnel confirmed that he suffered from depression. From his letters, the family knew he missed home.

It is hard to pinpoint the exact cause of depression. Some blame a chemical imbalance, and some say there's an abnormal cell connection.

After reading all of Burnette's letters and the family members' responses, I felt a sense of longing and sadness that I never got to know him. By writing this book, I want to honor him as well as others who have depression and can't find a way out. Through my book, I hope that you will look for God and find faith to see you through. If my work helps one person, I will feel elated.

Please pass these pages on to others. Please email me at dorisannvalentine@gmail.com with any comments.

Thank you. —Doris

I PRAY BECAUSE I'M INSPIRED BY THE GREAT CHRISTIAN APOLOGETIC.

> "I pray because I can't help myself. I pray because I'm helpless. I pray because the need flows out of me, all the time, walking and sleeping. It doesn't change God. It changes me." —C.S. Lewis

C.S. Lewis, "Jack" as he wanted to be called, was from an Irish background with a protestant minister father and a mathematician mother. He had an older brother named Warren. They were well to do, and the boys were exceptional students and adventurous playmates who enjoyed much love from their mom.

Suddenly, everything changed with the death of their mom when Jack was ten and Warren was twelve. Mrs. Lewis' death greatly affected Jack. His dad was despondent as well and shipped the boys off to a boarding school in London. Jack hated it and used his imagination to mentally remove himself from the solemn and stressful circumstances. He felt God had let him down. How could God allow his mom to die? When Jack turned sixteen, his dad signed him with a tutor who was an atheist. The tutor cemented Jack's despair and led him to becoming an atheist as well.

At seventeen years old Jack joined the army. He got out of the army healthy but still mad at God. He finally secured a position at Magdalen College, Oxford, as a professor. His ambition was to be a poet, but during this time he volunteered to talk on the radio to encourage others when war began again. He was so successful that this became a weekly thing. He employed his vivid imagination and began writing books. The exercise renewed faith in God. Some of his best-loved books, namely *The Lion, the Witch and the Wardrobe* of *The Chronicles of Narnia* seven-novel series, were and continue to be well read by children as well as adults across the world. Lewis applied themes of Christianity to these stories. He went on to write more books, which helped him work through his tough personal times.

I love his books and his quote about praying. Sometimes, I feel that I cannot help myself. Thoughts, questions, and messages just come over me to pray. And the prayers change me.

Here are other beloved quotes by Lewis: "Nothing that you have not given away will ever be really yours," and, "You are never too old to set another goal or to dream a new dream." Yes! Believe in yourself. God is not finished with you. I did not think that I would be writing a book at age 70.

Trust in God and pray that you can do what you have dreamed of doing. Let God sow the seed of greatness. Prayer is the most important key. Prayer unlocks all of the other keys, such as conscious awareness, to give heaven access. We are commanded to pray. Prayer is not an option for Christians. Pray, "If it's your will, Lord …."

Then thank him that it is already done. I have researched and read many authors with different opinions on the truth. Through the title *Why I Pray*, I want to touch on topics that are crucial for all people.

Doris A. Valentine

I PRAY TO UNDERSTAND HUMAN NATURE VS. THE SUPERNATURAL.

At the time of this writing, depression, worry, and fear are common problems we endure, as we all face a current crisis, a global pandemic that is wreaking havoc in the lives and economies of every nation on earth. Some people are afraid to step out of their houses for fear that they will contact this deadly virus. They have stayed isolated from relatives and friends. Back-to-back deadly shootings have occurred across the U.S. and major riots plague cities across our land.

The National Institute of Mental Health documents that the U.S. has at least 17.3 million adults who have had at least one major depressive episode. The breakdown is 7.1 % male and 8.7% female. This does not apply to sadness or grief, which are normal human emotions. This is major depression. The Institute is addressing major depression or depressive disorder, a diagnosable condition that's classified as a mood disorder which can bring long-lasting symptoms, such as overwhelming sadness, low energy, loss of appetite, and a lack of interest in activities that used to bring pleasure.

World Health Organization (WHO) estimates more than 300 million people worldwide suffer from depression. There have been more suicides during this pandemic than ever before. As of January 2021, National Institute of Mental Health claims suicides are the second leading cause of deaths between the ages of 10 to 34 and fourth among ages 34-54. In fact, there were more suicides (48,344) in US than homicides (18,830).

Centers for Disease Control and Prevention (CDC) facts show that for ages 15 to 24 the leading cause of suicide is depression. Depression, overall, affects 20-25% in any given year. Sadly, only one half of affected people seek treatment because they are ashamed or do not know how to ask for help.

We need to pray more and focus on our relationships with God. Proverbs 12:25 teaches, "Anxiety in the heart of man causes depression, But a good word makes it glad." In other words, the good word is any word that gives encouragement and relieves anxiety or depression.

It is important to note that many people suffer from chemical imbalances that require medication and/or clinical therapy for depression, anxiety, and other mood disorders. I do not discount their suffering. I do, however, encourage people who struggle on ANY level to use prayer to combat these issues. God understands this human frailty and, throughout the Bible, addresses it.

King Saul had depression. Prior to being king, he was chosen. He stood out. He was handsome, tall, and shy. Actually, he did not want to be king. Then when he became king, he felt the weight of everything. He became sad and depressed. In fact, he had David the shepherd boy play the lyre to entertain him and cheer him up. It made him feel better but then he would become angry and throw spears at David. David would flee. Saul then became what we today call paranoid. He was jealous of David, and tried his best to kill him. Yes, his depression and paranoia got the best of him. In his last battle he took his own life rather than let the enemy take him.

The pages that follow are my layman's attempt to share what I have learned in hopes that I can help anyone suffering from depression, worry, and fear.

Let us pray.

Dear Lord,

As best I know how and with the help and guidance of your Holy Spirit, I deliberately set my heart today to seek you, to serve you, to follow you, and to please you. Amen

WORRY

Worry will give way to unease, sending us down a path to anxiety and even depression. Worry allows one to dwell on difficulties or troubles. The Old English verb *wyrgan* meant "strangle." Another version of the term, from Middle English, is the word *warien*, meaning to twist, strain, or even grasp by the throat. In the Bible, worry is usually translated as anxiety or care. We often worry over things that we can do nothing about and things cannot even be sure about. According to the Bible, worry is concern over the unknown and uncontrollable future, and it tears us apart.

God has given us only today. Each day has enough trouble of its own (Mathew 6:34). Worry makes you feel worthless, forgotten, and unimportant. That's why Mathew 6:26 teaches, "Look at the birds of the air, for they neither sow nor reap nor gather into barns; yet your heavenly Father feeds them. Are you not of more value than they?" The birds enjoy what's there. If God is able to sustain the lesser creatures, won't he sustain the greater?

Mathew 6:31-34 reads, "Therefore do not worry, saying, 'What shall we eat?' or 'What shall we drink?' or 'What shall we wear?' For after all these things the Gentiles sought. Your heavenly Father knows that you need all these things. But seek first the kingdom of God and His righteousness, and all these things shall be added to you. Therefore, do not worry about tomorrow, for tomorrow will worry about its own things. Sufficient for the day *is* its own trouble." Pour out your attention on today. If you focus upon today, then energy is not wasted but efficiently used. You have energy left to solve problems. Jesus tells us to NOT be anxious about tomorrow, because those issues will most often take care of themselves. Focus on taking care of today's problems, only the troubles that you have to handle NOW, in order to eliminate worry.

We are commanded again and again not to worry. Concern is natural. Worry is human. Worry is also the failure to trust God. Trust God in the midst of storms. Storms are temporary. Allow storms to build you up. A calm sea never produces a good sailor. You are never remembered by what you avoided. You can plan for tomorrow but you must live by faith and action today. One who worries looks off into the future, but the future is not here yet. That is why worrying about the future tears us apart. Then in the 1600's, worry meant to bother, distress, or persecute. By the 1800's, the term meant to cause to feel anxious or distressed.

I PRAY FOR PERSPECTIVE.

Some popular authors write the following about worry:

> "Worry never robs tomorrow of its sorrow, it only zaps today of its joy." —Leo Buscaglia

> "The greatest mistake you can make in life is to be continually fearing you will make one."
> —Elbert Hubbard

> "Worry is like a rocking chair: it gives you something to do, but never gets you anywhere." —Erma Bombeck

> "Every tomorrow has two handles. We can take hold of it with the handle of anxiety or the handle of faith."
> —Henry Ward Beecher

The antidote for worry is worship through prayer. I believe the answer to *everything* is prayer. I believe God is as close as my next prayer.

From my research over the years, I found the following facts on the act of worrying:

- 40% of the things people worry about never happen
- 30% of our worries are related to past matters, which are now beyond our control
- 12% of our worries have to do with our health, even when we are not actually ill
- 10% of our worries are about friends and neighbors and are not based in evidence or fact
- Only 8% of our worries have some basis in reality, which means that over 90% of the things we worry about never happen.

David Jeremiah explains, "With all information in mind, try picturing the Christian prayer life as composed of three circles." The concept is illuminated through Philippians 4:6. The first is the Worry Circle, in which the word *nothing* is written because the Bible verse says, "Be anxious for nothing." The second is the Prayer Circle, in which the word *everything* is written because the verse says, "…let your requests be made known to God." The third is the Thanksgiving Circle, in which the word *anything* is written because the Bible says to pray "with thanksgiving." When we live within these three circles, we overcome the stress that comes into our lives.

Anxiety can enter every part of our lives. Beneath our anxiety is a need to feel in control. Control in any relationship is impossible. Let me say that again. Control in any relationship is impossible. Relationships are about give and take and actually releasing your control in exchange for connection. Our peace is found in knowing that the Creator of the universe holds us safely in the palm of his hand and will protect us no matter the situation in which we land. There are four Biblical methods by which one may relieve anxiety.

1. Rejoice in the Lord. Stand firm in the Lord.
2. Cultivate a gentle spirit.
3. Focus on the nearness of God. The Lord is with you always.
4. Plead with God in thankful prayer. Pray each morning before you rise and all day long as you feel anxious. Ask the lord to help you through any anxious moment.

Another one of my favorite authors is Charles Swindoll. In the devotional *Great Days with the Great Lives: Daily Insight from Great Lives of the Bible,* he writes, "I have never seen a habit just lie down, surrender, and die; we have to make a conscious effort if we hope to break longstanding habits. If you are negative today, chances are very good that when you wake up tomorrow morning you're still going to be negative. Force a vertical focus."

You should "… walk worthy of God who calls you into His own kingdom and glory" (1 Thessalonians 2:12). Ralph Waldo Emerson wrote, "Sorrow looks back, worry looks around, faith looks up." We all need to have faith in our heavenly father, believing that he works in our best interests. He created us and we are his people. Share your faith with others who are depressed or worried. Show them by reading his Word and living in a way that shows you believe that, through God, all things are possible.

You choose. Worry or pray. We all worry about our finances, our loved ones, our jobs, our health, and a host of other issues. It may be hard to relate to Jesus' words concerning worry. After all, Jesus had no children, no boss, and no bills to pay. Jesus never had to grocery shop for a family and make dollars stretch, or carpool kids to sports, try to make PTA meetings, and put dinner on the table. Jesus never had to take care of his elderly parents and help his teenagers plan for college at the same time. How can we apply his teaching about not worrying to life in this century?

Actually, these passages are more for us today than ever. In a materialistic, consumption-minded, technological world, Jesus tells us to order our priorities: "But seek the kingdom of God, and all these things shall be added to you" (Luke 12:31). For most of us, however, there is a large gap between managing our day-to-day activities and seeking God's kingdom.

In order to achieve the peace of God and to not be overwhelmed by the pressures of life, we have to change. Seventy percent of people do not like change. Change is good. Being concerned can be positive if it propels us into action. To seek first the kingdom means to pray first, releasing our fears and worries to the Lord. A change in behavior and in a particular attitude follows as we make some appropriate changes to our lifestyles. Taking some steps, even small ones, to change our lives will help us bridge the gap between worrying and operating in faith.

Over time, these adjustments will ultimately help us live in power, love, sound judgement, self-control, calm, and balance. On a practical note, the following list is a tool to help you as you work to resolve worry by relying on faith.

- Get facts and expert advice to prevent worrying unrealistically about a situation.
- Set deadlines to make decisions rather than ruminating forever.
- Limit worrying to a "worry list'" and take that list to the Lord in your daily Bible and prayer time.
- Delegate chores and other responsibilities.
- Give yourself permission to relax.
- Give yourself permission to make mistakes.
- Eat, sleep, and exercise properly.
- Try to see the humor in a situation, to keep a sense of perspective.
- De-clutter and organize, using calendars and to-do lists.
- Realize that you will not please everyone all of the time.
- Learn to say no. Ask yourself, "What's the worst that can happen-and is it likely to?"
- Mentally put your worries in a box with a lid and put them on the top shelf of your closet. No peeking!

Jesus modeled prayer when he went to the desert to fast and pray. Jesus also modeled action when he healed, taught, and followed God every step of the way. To be walking in peace, in calm, in trust, and in assurance is to find the balance of prayer and action, and eventually, freedom from worry.

Worry can be a time-consuming, almost obsessive, behavior. After all, every day brings new things to worry about! Worrying about every situation in life—whether big or small—will drive us to distraction. Not one problem is ever solved by worrying about it. In fact, many problems get worse because worry is immobilizing; thus, no action is taken to try to labor through the dilemma. Worry can thwart the work of the kingdom. "And which of you by worrying can add one cubit to his stature? If you then are not able to do the least, why are you anxious for the rest" (Luke 12:25-28)?

The definitions of prayer are as varied as the prayers we pray each day in moments of anxiety or moments of joy. Writer Anne Lamott professes that the two best prayers she knows are, "Help me, help me, help me," and "Thank you, thank you, thank you."

We have the perfect example in the prayer Jesus taught his disciples in Mathew 6:9-13 and in Luke 11:2.

In this manner, therefore, pray:
Our Father in heaven,
Hallowed be Your name.
Your kingdom come.
Your will be done
On earth as it is in heaven.
Give us this day our daily bread.
And forgive us our debts,
As we forgive our debtors.
And do not lead us into temptation,
But deliver us from the evil one.
For yours is the kingdom and the power and the glory
  forever. Amen.

Why Pray? Regardless of the form or words we use, it is important that we pray because prayer nourishes our souls much as food nourishes our bodies. The act of praying gives us sacred space aside from our daily, secular responsibilities to imagine ourselves as God sees us and to rest, when weary, in the safety and peace of God's arms.

In Psalms, we learn that God did not remove all of David's troubles, even though David cried out for God to do so. We are not to treat God as a genie in a lamp who grants all our whims and wishes.

Sometimes God takes us out of our trouble, but more often he stands *with* us and walks *with* us through adversity. God always answers when his children cry out to him.

Every good father does. He may not answer us the way we want to be answered, but he always answers.

God will often give strength, or confidence, in our souls to help us face our troubles. Boldness and strength come not because we get everything we want at the exact moment we ask for it but because God is in charge.

Psalm 139 stands out to me. Verses 23-24 are a wonderful prayer, if you will. "Search me, O God, and know my heart; Try me, and know my anxieties; And see if *there is any* wicked way in me, And lead me in the way everlasting."

DEPRESSION, ANXIETY, AND FEAR

We have volumes of books on the subjects. Countless doctors treat people for these three afflictions. We also have a Bible that gives us instructions to help us cope with these negative responses. One commonly used acronym for fear is False Evidence Appearing Real. Some version of the phrase "Do not fear" is in the Bible 365 times for a reason. Oswald Chambers stated, "The remarkable thing about God is that, when you fear God, you fear nothing else; whereas, if you do not fear God, you fear everything else."

We must pray with our eyes on God and not on difficulties. Our fears are chains but only while we empower them. Don't underestimate your courage. If necessary, face troubles in stages and gain strength from your progress. Often our fear is outdated or based on misunderstanding. Challenge your fears. Break their spell and you're free. Learn from Mark Twain, who wrote, "Courage is the mastery of fear, not the absence of fear."

No healthy Christian ever chooses suffering. Instead, he chooses God's will, as Jesus did, whether or not God's will allows for suffering. The life of faith is not a life of mounting up with wings but a life of walking and not fainting (Isaiah 40:31). We invite Christ into our hearts. Then we talk to God with undivided attention. Pray, giving thanks to God, and take time to come into his presence.

When fear comes to mind, recite David's words in Psalm 27:1-4: "The LORD *is* my light and my salvation; Whom shall I fear? The LORD *is* the strength of my life; Of whom shall I be afraid? ... One *thing* I have desired of the LORD, That will I seek: That I may dwell in the house of the LORD All the days of my life...."

ANXIETY

Anxiety has a root of fear; when we worry, we allow fear to impose itself on our view of tomorrow. We have no idea what tomorrow truly holds, yet we imagine the worst and are filled with care and concern- We worry. How much better to hold fast to faith! We should grab hold of the truth of who God is and the promises God has made. Faith recognizes no trial is greater than God's ability and reliability to always do exactly as he says; God is faithful to live out his Word unfailingly.

Rather than allow doubt to create *anxiety* within us, we should always talk to God about all of our needs. Though trials come, we can find thankfulness in recalling all that our God has promised us in his Word. We can hold to those truths and take all our concerns to him, knowing he will always hear and always meet our needs.

Pray, "Father, help me leave anxiety behind and hold fast to faith in you."

Doris A. Valentine

SELF-TALK

Another way to relieve worry, depression, anxiety, and fear is through self-talk. Say to yourself any of the following: "Today I will love people as they are." "Today I will love someone who does not love me." "Today I will try to make it easier for others to love me." "Today I will take along some extra love."

Philippians 4:6-7 reminds us, "Be anxious for nothing, but in everything by prayer and supplication, with thanksgiving, let your requests be made known to God; [7] and the peace of God, which surpasses all understanding, will guard your hearts and minds through Christ Jesus." In 2 Timothy 1:7, we learn, " For God has not given us a spirit of fear, but of power and of love and of a sound mind." In John 14:27, we know, "Peace I leave with you, My peace I give to you; not as the world gives do I give to you. Let not your heart be troubled, neither let it be afraid."

I pray because it strengthens my relationship with God. In the same way that our friendships and relationships with people need communication to be strengthened, so does our relationship with God. He has blessed us with the ability to speak with him at all times, *whenever* we need him. No matter how we come to the Lord, whether to present our requests or to sit silently in his presence, We can trust that he hears us. It can help if we just say this prayer: "Lord Jesus, I am often worried about many things. I worry about tomorrow, about my family, about what friends are really thinking, about health, about clothes, about money, and about countless other meaningless things. Jesus, I know that my worry will do nothing, but the thoughts are rooted in my mind, and I know I cannot remove them without your help. Remind me of your provision. Show me ways to let go of my worry. Please grant me with a heart like David who sang your praises and exalted your name in poetry. Amen"

The Serenity Prayer is a beautiful poem/prayer to say and repeat. There are many versions in books and online. This is how I recite this wonderful petition.

God, grant me the serenity to accept the things I cannot change,
Courage to change the things I can,
And wisdom to know the difference.

(Most only know this part, but the prayer continues.)

Living one day at a time,
Enjoying one moment at a time,
Accepting hardship as the pathway to peace,
Taking, as Jesus did,
This sinful world as it is, not as I would have it,
Trusting that he will make all things right if I surrender to His will;
That I may be reasonably happy in this life,
And supremely happy with Him forever in the next.
Amen.

Doris A. Valentine

The prayer is attributed to an America Theologian from the early 1930's by the name of Reinhold Niebuhr. In my research, I found two other men accredited as well. One was the 18th century theologian Friedrich Oetinger. The other was a philosopher in 500 AD named Boethius who wrote similar prayers. This most famous prayer was made popular by Alcoholics Anonymous during the 20th century.

This is a prayer of acceptance of hardships, a prayer of trust in God that he will bring peace and happiness. The ending echoes life everlasting and Christians' belief in the hope of eternity. The word *serenity* means a place where we are calm, peaceful, and free from stress. The Apostle Paul writes in 2 Corinthians 12:9-10, "And He said to me, 'My grace is sufficient for you, for My strength is made perfect in weakness.' Therefore most gladly I will rather boast in my infirmities, that the power of Christ may rest upon me. Therefore I take pleasure in infirmities, in reproaches, in needs, in persecutions, in distresses, for Christ's sake. For when I am weak, then I am strong."

Weakness/pain does not have to be our enemy. Paul experienced a great revelation from God. To keep him from being "exalted above measure," however, he had was given a "thorn in the flesh." Most likely this was some physical ailment that constantly bothered him. Many people face chronic pain or physical afflictions. They may think that if God would heal them, they would be much more valuable and effective in ministry. But God's power is often best revealed when he works through human weakness. His "strength is made perfect in weakness."

SAINT FRANCIS OF ASSISI

Here is another prayer/poem/song that can be used to encourage others and sometimes is used in funerals. It was written by Saint Francis of Assisi. It reads:

Lord, make me an instrument of your peace; where there is hatred, let me sow love; where there is injury, pardon; where there is doubt, faith; where there is despair, hope; where there is darkness, light; and where there is sadness, joy.

O Divine Master, Grant that I may not so much seek to be consoled as to console; to be understood as to understand; to be loved as to love. For it is in giving that we receive, it is in pardoning that we are pardoned, and it is in dying that we are born to eternal life.

Saint Francis of Assisi was baptized as Giovanni, then renamed Francesco di Pietro di Bernardone. He was born in the small town of Assisi, Italy, in the year 1108. He came from the wealthy family of a luxury clothmaker. The book *Reluctant Saint* by Donald Spoto is an informative read on Saint Francis' life. To summarize, he was very handsome, well liked, and in his twenties ran with a group of young men who played pranks on people. Being the leader, he was called the "King of the Rebels." War broke out in 1202 with the neighboring town, and Saint Francis joined the war and was captured. He stayed in prison for a year, suffered from malaria, and was finally released after family gave a ransom.

Because of this dark dungeon life, he aimlessly wandered until he came upon a church in ill repair. There he heard the voice of God.

Saint Francis renounced his family and wealth. From that time on, he chose to live a life of poverty. He founded the Franciscan orders of the Friars Minor, the women's Order of St. Clare, and the lay Third Order. He was canonized two years after his death by Pope Gregory IX in July 1228 because of his devotion to solitude, prayer, helping the poor, and raising money to rebuild rundown churches. Some call him the Patron Saint of Birds and Animals.

As Christians we need to look at the suffering of many past saints, disciples, and apostles to see the lives that they *chose* to see that our lives are not half as bad as we think.

> "Great eagles fly alone; great lions hunt alone, great souls walk alone-alone with God."
> —Leonard Ravenhill

God says in Hebrews 13:5, "I will never leave you nor forsake you." God is always there through all of our trials and temptations. Tap into the goodness of God. Take these burdens off your shoulders and give them up to God. Pray each day, hopefully in the morning, to get your day right and ask for his help. He has promised if your truly believe and ask that everything will be given unto you. It may not be in your time but in God's time. Let him help you. Praise him for the mercy he has shown you. Charles Swindoll says it best: "Instead of living in the grip of fear, held captive by the chains of tension and dread, when we release our preoccupation with worry, we find God's hand at work on our behalf. He, our 'God of Peace,' comes to our aid, changing people, releasing tension, altering difficult circumstances. The more you practice giving your mental burdens to the Lord, the more exciting it gets to see how God will handle the things that are impossible for you to do anything about."

"For He Himself is our peace…." Ephesians 2:14

Doris A. Valentine

THE PRAYER OF JABEZ

The Prayer of Jabez is a most familiar prayer. Many authors have written about it. In 1 Chronicles 4:9-10, we learn, "Now Jabez was more honorable than his brothers, and his mother called his name Jabez, saying, 'Because I bore *him* in pain.' And Jabez called on the God of Israel saying, 'Oh, that You would bless me indeed, and enlarge my territory, that Your hand would be with me, and that You would keep *me* from evil, that I may not cause pain!' So God granted him what he requested."

Who was Jabez? He appears only in the Old Testament in 1 Chronicles as a minor figure. He is implied to be ancestor of the Kings of Judah, although he is not explicitly included in the lineage. Jabez' birth is difficult and for this reason his mother named him Jabez, which means "pain" or "he makes sorrowful." Jabez, who probably suffered from low self-esteem caused by the label his own mother gave him, broke through the wrong identity given to him. He did so by calling on God.

Think about that for a moment. Some of us suffer being called names by the people around us. They may label us according to how they receive us. That's exactly what Jabez went through. Imagine your own mother giving you a name that is a lifelong label. Thankfully, as the Bible verse says, despite the label or identity given him, Jabez broke through and became "more honorable than his brothers." He rose above any label.

I think that Jabez' story teaches us we can rise above any situation. How? He called upon God for help. You can too. God is able to turn things around for us even when the world or people are against us. God can lift us up and cause us to be a blessing to all. The Bible gives us hope. That is why I pray. How about you?

Doris A. Valentine

WHY PRAY

If you pray with a believing and contrite heart, God will answer your prayer. He can deliver you through dark parts of your life. He is always there. Just reach out. Lean on him. Go to him in prayer.

Why do we pray? We pray to develop an intimacy with our God. A Scottish teacher, Oswald Chambers, said this about prayer: "We tend to use prayer as a last resort, but God wants it to be our first line of defense." We should wake up every morning and pray, thanking God and asking for his forgiveness.

Find a quiet place for your daily time with God in the morning. Wait, watch, and listen. Make it a habit. In Mathew 16:24, Jesus stated, "If anyone desires to come after Me, let him deny himself, and take up his cross, and follow Me." Jesus said this to his disciples and followers. We must put God first and be willing to suffer anything for his sake. The more we follow Christ, the more we become changed. When we deny ourselves, it allows God to use us for his purposes.

On controlling our tongues, James 3:8 teaches, " But no man can tame the tongue. *It is* an unruly evil, full of deadly poison." Several years ago, Bible commentary writer Nicky Gumbel said, "The words of the tongue should have three gatekeepers: Is it true? Is it kind? Is it necessary?" Although a small organ of the body, the tongue has the power to cause happiness and joy or heartache and sorrow. The book of

James was written to encourage early Christians to live a Christlike life. In James 3:3, the writer uses an analogy of how a small bit in the horse's mouth restrains the mighty beast. James 3:4 tells how a small rudder controls a great ship, even in storms and fierce winds. The tongue is a lesser member of the body, yet it wields great power. James said the tongue is the key factor in controlled living. If we control our tongues we can have power over other parts of our bodies.

Doris A. Valentine

WORDS

An unkind word can be quite meaningful. I come from a family of critics who sometimes told me I wasn't smart. Friends told me I was too skinny. To this day I remember in detail those insults and how they affected me. We need to practice the golden rule of, "Do to others as you would like them to do to you" (Luke 6:31 NLT). I like the adage, "If you have nothing good to say about a person, don't say anything at all."

What if you walked into your job today committed to being the best you can be by helping others be their best? I know. That sounds unnatural and just about the last thing you'd ever decide to do on your way to work. It feels more normal to look out for yourself and say, "Phooey on everyone else." Many of us are selfish this way. The practice of giving to others what they need to succeed is pure Jesus. He constantly reminded his followers to give themselves to one another without hesitation or guile.

The difficulty of the lesson was magnified by the fact that it ran against their competitive nature, as it does today. Thus, Jesus had to deal with disciples whose only goal seemed to be winning his favor rather than serving one another. Jesus made his disciples feel special by performing many services, such as washing their feet, feeding them, teaching them through parables, and giving them special powers. Many people aren't treated nicely by superiors, so they will notice any effort you make in the direction of Jesus-like kindness.

Mary Kay Ash, founder of Mary Kay cosmetics, said her key to working with people was imagining they're wearing placards that say, "Make me feel special." She proceeded in doing that, and her success certifies her leadership advice. Help others be their personal best.

Doris A. Valentine

MOTHER TERESA

I pray to feel the essence of god's love and live Jesus' sacrifice. Feeling special or loved brings Sister Mother Teresa to mind. Most noted for her work in Calcutta, India, Mother Teresa started each day in communion with Jesus and then went out with her Rosary beads to find and serve him. She cared for the unwanted, the unloved, and the ignored. She formed the Co-Workers of Mother Teresa and Sick and the Suffering Co-Workers. These groups were and are comprised of people from many faiths and nationalities who share her spirit of prayer, her simplicity, her heart for sacrifice, and her apostolate of humble works of love.

    A little about her background: Mother Teresa was a Catholic nun who became an international ambassador for Jesus. She left a testament of unshakable faith, invincible hope, and extraordinary charity. Her response to Jesus's plea, "Come be my light," was to be a symbol of compassion to the world and a living witness to the thirsting love of God. You can learn more in her wonderful book *Come Be My Light: The Private Writings of the Saint of Calcutta.*

Here are some of her famous quotes:

I alone cannot change the world, but I can cast a stone across the waters to create many ripples.

Not all of us can do great things. But we can do small things with great love.

It is easy to love the people far away. It is not always easy to love those close to us. It is easier to give a cup of rice to relieve hunger than to relieve the loneliness and pain of someone unloved in our own home. Bring love into your home for this is where our love for each other must start.

Life is an opportunity, benefit from it.
Life is a beauty, admire it.
Life is bliss, taste it.
Life is a dream, realize it.
Life is a challenge, meet it.
Life is a duty, complete it.
Life is a game, play it.
Life is costly, care for it.
Life is wealth, keep it.
Life is love, enjoy it.
Life is mystery, know it.
Life is a promise, fulfill it.
Life is a sorrow, overcome it.
Life is a song, sing it.
Life is a struggle, accept it.
Life is a tragedy, confront it.
Life is an adventure, dare it.
Life is luck, make it.
Life is too precious, do not destroy it.
Life is Life, fight for it!

Mother Teresa caught the imagination of the world not because she is a great writer or theologian but because she was a person of immense compassion and openness. For Mother Teresa, her lifelong habit of quieting her ego through prayer led to a vibrant life in the world and the rich development of her personality. A loss of self leads to the discovery of soul.

Prayer is turning your heart and your mind to God. If we don't pray, our presence will have no power. Our words will have no power. As Mother Teresa said, "For knowledge of God produces love, and knowledge of the self produces humility." Knowledge of the self is also a safeguard against pride, especially when you are tempted in life.

Prayer, to be fruitful, must come from the heart and must be able to touch the heart of God. Jesus taught his disciples to pray, "Our Father." God looks at his hands, which he used to carve us. "See, I have inscribed you on the palms of My hands; Your walls are continually before Me" (Isaiah 49:16). He looks at his hands and sees us there. How wonderful the tenderness and love of God!

If we pray the "Our Father" and live it, we will be holy. Everything is there: God, myself, my neighbor. *If* we forgive, then we can pray and be holy. All of this comes from a humble heart, and if we have this we will know how to love God, to love self, and to love our neighbors. Mother Teresa also said, "Every human being comes from the hand of God, and we all know something of God's love for us. Whatever our religion, we know that if we really want to love, we must first learn to forgive before anything else."

Our words will be useless unless they come from a Christian spirit within us. Words that do not shine the light of Christ increase the darkness. Today, more than ever, we need to pray for the light, to know the will of God, for the love to accept the will of God, and for the way to do the will of God. Jesus also taught us to be meek and humble of heart. Neither of these can we do unless we know what silence is. Both humility and prayer grow from an ear, mind, and tongue that have lived in silence with God, for in the silence of the heart God speaks.

Mother Teresa's Prayer:
Lord when I am hungry, give me someone needing food. When I am thirsty, send me someone needing a drink. When I am cold, send me someone to warm. When I am grieved, send me someone to console. When my cross grows heavy let me carry another's cross too. When I am poor, lend me someone in need. When I have no time, give me someone I can help a little while. When I am humiliated, let me have someone to praise. When I am disheartened, send me someone to cheer. When I need understanding give me someone who needs mine. When I need to be looked after give me someone to care for. When I think only of myself draw my thoughts to another."

Pray: *Father God, I pray that I have Mother Teresa's heart for love and that you will come into me and help me to share my love to all within my family and neighborhood. Amen.*

I PRAY TO LEARN FROM GOD'S WORK IN OTHERS.

Charles de Foucauld stated, "The moment I realized that God existed, I knew that I could not do otherwise than to live for him alone…Faith strips the mask from the world and reveals God in everything. It makes nothing impossible and renders meaningless such words as anxiety, danger, and fear, so that the believer goes through life calmly and peacefully, with profound joy—like a child, hand in hand with his mother." Charles de Foucauld lived from 1858 to 1916. He was born into a wealthy French family. He lost his mother and father and his bearings after being orphaned at the age of six. He was raised by his grandfather.

Charles de Foucauld joined the military at an early age, just as his grandfather had. He was a cavalry officer, explorer, and geographer. In an operation in Morocco, he studied the faith of the Muslim people. Through that experience, he began to understand his own. He became a Catholic priest and hermit who took a vow of poverty, living with the Tuareg people in Sahara in Algeria. He said, "Every Christian must be an apostle, this is not a counsel, it is a commandment. My apostolate must be an apostolate of goodness. On seeing me people should say to themselves, since this man is so good, his religion must be good. And if I am asked why I am so gentle and good I must reply, because I am the servant of the One whose goodness is still greater. If only you knew how good my Master Jesus is!"

About prayer, he said, "Prayer is just conversation with God: listening to him; speaking with him; gazing upon him in silence. The best prayer is the one in which there is the most love. Adoration, wordless admiration, that is the most eloquent form of prayer: that wordless admiration which contains the most passionate declaration of love…."

God puts people in our lives all of the time to help us with our journeys through this life. We need to pray for something and be persistent. Just keep on praying. Keith Green wrote a song called "Make my life a prayer to you." So who was Keith Green? He was eleven years old when he went on the *I've Got A Secret* TV series with host Steve Allen and four famous panelists. Green's secret was that he had written several songs and signed a five-year rock and roll recording contract with Decca (one of the largest recording companies at the time). He was hugely talented. He was an Elton John on the piano with so much charisma and showmanship plus a beautiful voice and songwriting talent.

Green came from a Jewish family, but as a young adult he felt he was going nowhere. He lived in California during the hippie age of the 1970s, when everyone was trying to "find himself." He went through drugs and religions trying to find what was missing in his life. He sang and played at a bar called Blah Blah Blah. There, he earned rave reviews of his talent. He had a bad experience with Mescaline (a hallucinogen derived from Peyote) and decided drugs held no meaning.

Not long after that, he was persuaded to go to a Bible study group by a friend. This encounter with people who loved Jesus turned Green's whole world around. He realized that Jesus was the only way and that he is our Lord and Savior. His wife Melody and he decided to give their lives to Christ. As he did with his music and other life choices, Green jumped in head first to proclaim Jesus. He was so adamant about professing his faith that he turned a lot of people off. He signed with Sparrow, a religious recording company. Green and Melody wrote gospel music. In California, they started helping the homeless and giving them a place to live. So convicted, Green dropped his recording company and gave free concerts. He had a list of over 6000 people wanting his record albums, which he gave away for whatever anyone was able to pay. Sometimes he and Melody received a dollar and sometimes $5,000.

Because of lack of space and residence ordinances, the Greens moved from California to Texas where they had lots of land and started the Last Days Ministries. They and their four children lived there until Green and two of his small children were killed in a plane crash. Melody resides in California and continues to work with Christian ministries.

Just as Jesus used Keith, Jesus uses us and our lives to help people who are anxious, worried, or depressed. You can help others in your own area of influence. Say this prayer: *Father, Help me to be a good Christian who helps others to learn more about you and to do good works in your name. We know, Lord Jesus, we can plant and water, but you are the one who saves. Amen.*

Doris A. Valentine

I PRAY BECAUSE IT IS A HUMBLE AND THANKFUL TRADITION TO SEEK GOD FIRST.

Our forefathers used prayer when writing the constitution. Every important event in our nation's early history was founded upon a strong faith in God and fervent prayer. For example:

- The Continental Congress called for a day of fasting and prayer in the colonies in 1775 when it became clear that they would need to fight in order to free themselves from England's rule. God answered their prayers.
- The men who drew up and signed the Declaration of Independence believed they were establishing America as a Christian nation and relied on God to help them draft this document. Because they wanted it to reflect their faith in God, they specifically stated their belief that "…all men are created equal, that they are endowed by their Creator with certain unalienable rights."
- The American Congress declared a Day of Fasting and Prayer during the War of 1812. God answered the nation's prayers with many miracles. I believe that if God had not acted in favor of the American Army, the British could have won the war.

- During the drawing up of the Constitution, all of the men involved under George Washington's leadership found themselves disagreeing on some issues. It seemed that they had reached an impasse. Then Benjamin Franklin stepped forward to remind the men of all the miracles God had done on their behalf when they battled for their independence. He said, "I have lived ⋯ a long time, and the longer I live, the more convincing proofs I see of this truth - that god governs in the affairs of men. And if a sparrow cannot fall to the ground without his notice, is it probable that an empire can rise without his aid?" He then called the men to prayer every morning that they were together. After their very first morning of prayer, the air was cleared, and they were able to come to agreement. They created a document that has kept our nation strong for over two hundred years. They were certain they could not have succeeded without guidance from God.

During the Civil War, President Abraham Lincoln called for a National Day of Fasting And Prayer in order to confess the nation's sins of slavery and pride and then repent of them. The believers in this movement then acknowledged God's goodness to them and humbly asked for his forgiveness. Within two days after that day of prayer, everything turned around and paved the way for victory, the preservation of the Union, and the freeing of the slaves.

There are countless examples throughout the history of our nation when leaders called people to pray in hopeless situations. We have often taken for granted the direct results of the power of a praying nation. God is the same today as he was then. He promises in 2 Chronicles 7:14, "… if My people who are called by My name will humble themselves, and pray and seek My face, and turn from their wicked ways, then I will hear from heaven, and will forgive their sin and heal their land." God is saying that to us today. What a powerful nation we could have if we were a wholly praying nation.

These are words we cannot afford to ignore. Only God can help us get rid of evil and protect us from threats to our safety. Only God can unify us and put us on the right path. But we have to do our part and humbly come to God in prayer.

I PRAY FOR OTHERS AND MYSELF.

In his book *When God Prays*, Skip Heitzig suggests that we learn to use "straight talk" with God. He offers these simple requests: *Keep me, Lord; Teach me, Lord;* and *Send me, Lord.* In the same way that Jesus asked his Father not to remove his disciples from the world but to keep them safe, I encourage you to pray for yourself, your Christian friend, your family, pastors, and leaders.

Thank God for your present position in life, your occupation, family, school, career, home, neighborhood, state, and country. Reflect on God's promise to you, such as those contained in the following verses:

> Romans 8:28 "And we know that all things work together for good to those who love God, to those who are the called according to *His* purpose."

> Psalm 32:8 "I will instruct you and teach you in the way you should go; I will guide you with My eye."

Doris A. Valentine

It isn't easy to trust God in times of adversity. Feelings of distress, despair, and darkness trouble our souls as now, just as they troubled all of the sinners and saints in these pages and throughout history. We sometimes wonder if God truly cares about our plight. But not to trust him is to doubt his sovereignty and to question his goodness. In order to trust God we must view our adverse circumstances through eyes of faith, not in our senses. Hebrews 10:39 emboldens us, "But we are not of those who [shrink back and are destroyed], but of those who believe to the saving of the soul."

God has placed you where you are for his own purposes. Thank him for all of the blessings he has poured out on your life. Ask God to take you to a new depth of faith, where his love and mercy will keep you safe from the raging storms of life. God is our refuge and strength, always ready to help in times of trouble. Lean on the Lord and his Word to see you through all trials and temptations.

ABOUT THE AUTHOR

Doris A. Valentine grew up in Sevier County and graduated from Sevier County High School in 1968. She went to college at The University of Tennessee in Knoxville, where she met and married Mickey Valentine and became a school teacher in Knoxville and later Spring Branch, Texas, and Fort Lauderdale, Florida. The Valentines have children Alison, Sean, and Kristofer. After retiring from teaching, they returned to Tennessee. She taught Sunday school and story time to young children throughout the community. Doris always had a desire to write, from penning poems in high school to songs and inspirational books throughout adulthood. Readers may reach Doris at DorisAnnValentine@gmail.com.

From Doris: *One of my favorite verses is Isaiah 40:31: "But those who trust in the* LORD *will find new strength. They will soar high on wings like eagles. They will run and not grow weary. They will walk and not faint." This speaks to me and tells me God has the capacity to empower those who are weary if they will trust Him. Amen. I hope you enjoy this book.*

www.ingramcontent.com/pod-product-compliance
Lightning Source LLC
Chambersburg PA
CBHW031948070426
42453CB00007BA/506